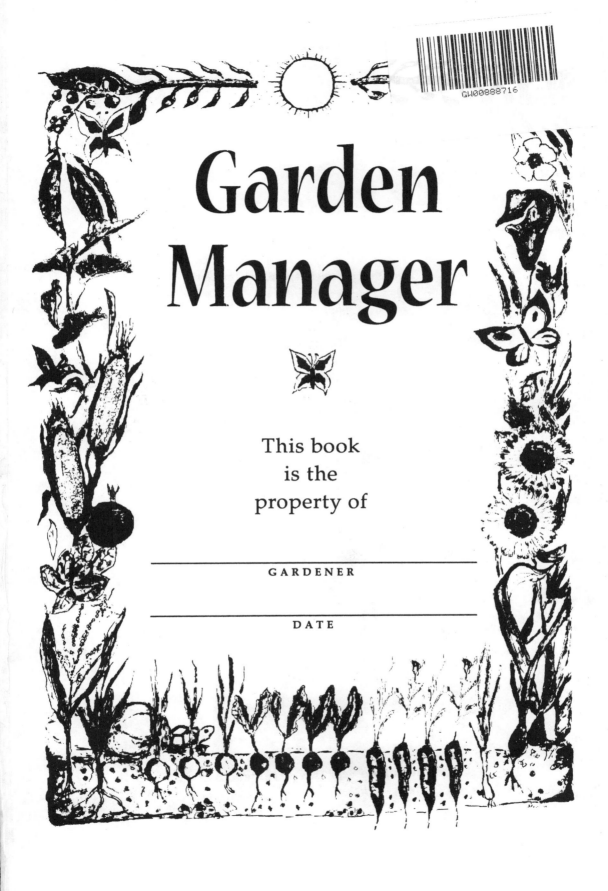

Garden Manager

This book
is the
property of

_____

GARDENER

_____

DATE

Marlor
Press
Books

London for the Independent Traveler

Garden Manager

*New York for the Independent Traveler**

Complete Trip Diary

Going Abroad

The Other Side of Sydney

State by State Guide to Budget Motels

*Winner of the **Best Travel Guidebook Award**
from *Publisher's Marketing Association*

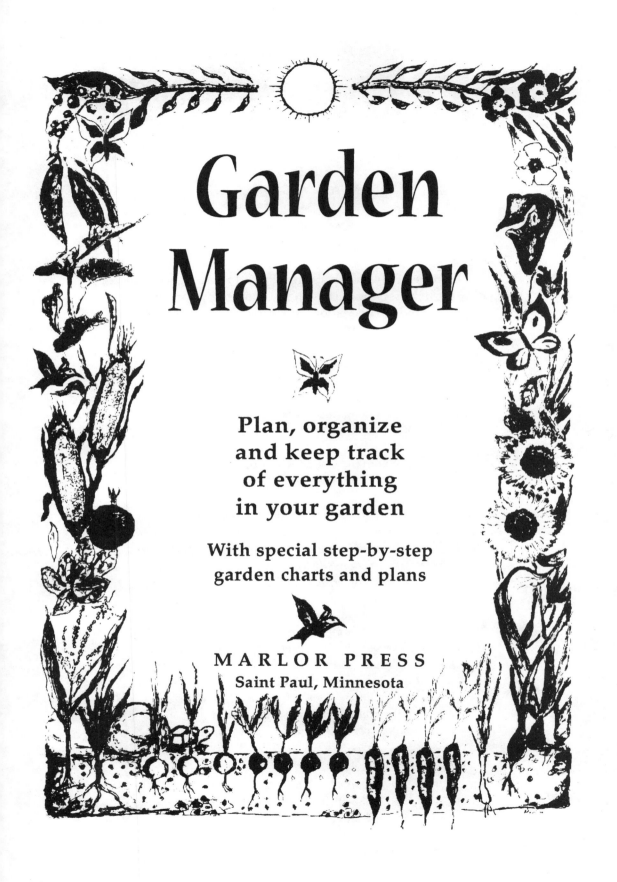

Garden
Manager

Plan, organize
and keep track
of everything
in your garden

With special step-by-step
garden charts and plans

MARLOR PRESS
Saint Paul, Minnesota

GARDEN MANAGER

Copyright 1998
MARLOR PRESS

Illustrations by Marlin Bree

With special thanks to those who contributed
gardening information and hints,
including Alice Gratke and Leah Peterson

Printed in the United States of America
ISBN 0-943400-96-1

MARLOR PRESS, INC
4304 Brigadoon Drive
Saint Paul, MN 55126

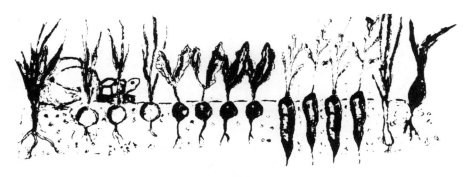

CONTENTS

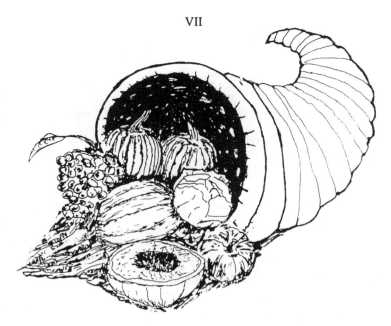

ABOUT
THIS
BOOK

**Nature gives to every time and season
some beauties of its own. — Charles Dickens**

YOUR *GARDEN MANAGER* is a year-around *working* book. It is for all types of gardeners — experienced to just beginning —and for use in developing all sorts of gardens.

Write in it as you wish, erase in it — and even tear out pages. By all means, take it to the garden with you. Toss it on your work-table. You'll find its lay-flat soft-cover design lets you write in it easily.

If you use a ball or fiber-tipped pen, be certain not to use water-soluble inks. If a bit of mist, rain or water gets on your work, the ink may smudge or run and possibly ruin your permanent entries.

Tabs can help you organize your work. You can purchase some tabs or create your own tabs on yellow gummed pieces of paper. These stick out from the side of a page, marking a section. Write your own headings. For example, you can tab *Planting Plan*, which tells what crops you planted as well as *Permanent Planting Information*, which contains information about your plants or seeds (just in case you lost the seed packet or nursery's tag.) Now you can flip back and forth easily between the two tabbed sections.

If you work with the *Garden Manager* for just a few minutes at a time, you'll find it will be packed with useful information. It will not only help you understand your garden or plantings better and help you produce better results — but you also will get more enjoyment from the time you spend gardening.

Getting organized

THIS BOOK is a five-year, all-season master workbook to help you plan, organize, and keep track of everything you plant. It can be begun at any time, for any type of garden, and used all year around.

It is divided into the gardening season's four cycles:

1/ Getting ready to plant
2/ Planting
3/ Harvest
4/ Season's end

1 Getting ready to plant lets you prepare for the season ahead — and dream a little about your next garden. Here you can begin your planning, determine what you will need, and make plans to order supplies. Here you will find: *Supplier's Names and Addresses: An Organizer*, for plant and seed producers or suppliers, equipment retailers, and others on which you want to keep a record. Next you can plan your purchases in *Ordering*. It's an easy way to keep track of what you ordered, when, and what it cost you. This record and organizer will be useful not only throughout the season — but in years to come as you refer back to it. It can save you time and money.

2 Planting lets you plan what you want to grow. Special *Garden Grid Plans* make it fun to visualize and easy to lay out your garden or plantings not only for the coming season but from year to year. Here you can organize a *Planting Plan* with the crops you ordered, the date planted and estimated maturity. In *Permanent Planting Information*, you have a permanent record of the information from each seed packet or bulb. This includes the plant name, row information, estimated maturity in days, and important instructions for care, thinning and harvesting (or reharvesting). This is **important** basic information kept permanently — with no anguish over missing or misplaced seed packets or growing instructions.

Gardening is food for the soul

3 **Harvest.** Here's the fulfillment of your efforts. You can analyze and record the results of your season's gardening and total up your overall harvest or evaluate your gardon's blooms. You can also log anything that may have affected your garden, good or bad. You can gain valuable insights into your gardening — important for future plans.

4 **Season's End** lets you jot down your observations, including what you want to change next year for better results or what plants you have had outstanding results with and want to work with again. You can begin deciding what you want to do to make next year's garden even better and more fun.

Using this book

THE GARDEN MANAGER is an invaluable management tool for any creative gardener — beginner or advanced — whether you are an occasional gardener with a small plot in the backyard, or a dedicated master gardener developing the New American Garden, with different specialty gardens for flowers, herbs and vegetables.

Within its pages, you plan and organize your gardening through a complete gardening cycle, from when you first select your seeds through final maturity. By keeping records over several seasons, you can do a better job of planning, with better timing, for more consistent results.

This helps you bring an important continuity to your gardening efforts. Your records will be in one central organizer, so you will not have to rely on elusive memory for such important decisions as whether or not to plant a specific crop at a certain time, or whether to repeat your purchase of a seed that did not do well for you. Basically, you can do more of what you did well — and eliminate those things that didn't turn out so well.

Best of all, your *Garden Manager* will become an important link between you and your garden throughout the year. You'll find that your skills, as well as your gardening results, will grow in direct proportion to the time you spend with your book.

Fact: Gardening is one of the
top outdoor activities for adults

Gardening: A perspective

YOU WILL FIND that working with your own *Garden Manager* is
personally satisfying. As you jot down your notes, you might be
reminded of what a famous novelist once observed: Writing lets us
"taste life *twice* — first in the *living* of it, then in the *telling*."

With this book, we enter a process by which we focus on an aspect of
our lives which we love with more clarity and detail. It's a discovery
— of the world about us — and of *ourselves*.

As our words continue through the pages, season after season, we
can live again in the pages we have kept, recalling many fine
memories of past gardens and experience. By writing things down,
we also keep a record for others who follow in generations to come.

It is a process that can extend to others. Keeping a *Garden Manager*
can lead to many happy talks and family projects, such as growing
special plants or flowers, with family members developing their own
garden space. Your interest in gardening ultimately may lead you
and your family to special projects, such as trips to famous gardens
or outstanding gardening efforts in this country and abroad. A love
of nature and gardening is a good gift to pass on to all in the family.

For the love of gardening

PART OF OUR ENORMOUS satisfaction with gardening comes from
our awareness of its continuous changes. We see changes in
plants, once just seeds, now growing green and blossoming. If you
listen carefully, the rustle of the breeze through your garden almost
sings of promise.

We feel a special kinship and sense a special stewardship
over this plot of ground. We have made it our own world,
and, on some very good days, we know not only the sights and
sounds but even the very feel of our garden.

Our most primitive and most sophisticated senses somehow come
alive. We not only become a little closer to the world of nature and all
that is fine within it, but in the process, we also come a little closer to
ourselves.

Idea: Plant a kid's garden

SECTION 1

GETTING
READY

- 🌷 Suppliers' names & addresses:
  a gardener's organizer

- 🌷 Garden ordering record

- 🌷 Garden notes

SUPPLIER'S NAMES AND ADDRESSES: AN ORGANIZER

Take time for all things that grow.

THIS IS A HANDY ORGANIZER to keep the names, addresses and telephone numbers (fax numbers, too) of your major suppliers so that you quickly can get in touch with them for an order, a question, or possibly the return of a plant. You can add Web and E-mail addresses as well.

The organizer is divided into three sections:

1/ Garden **plant & seed suppliers**
2/ Garden **equipment retailers** and
3/ **Miscellaneous**, which can include soil testing firms, university extension division specialists, or other advisors or suppliers you use.

An example of how to use your organizer:

1/ PLANT & SEED SUPPLIERS

Name _Flowering Gardens Co._
Address _123 Blossom Blvd._
City _Big Bulb_ State _MN_ Zip _43210_
Telephone _(215) 123-4567_ Fax _(215) 123-5432_
Web address _www. floweringarden . com_
E-mail _daisy @ floweringarden . com_
Comments: _Order $25 or more to_
get 3 free plants. Double bonus
if order by April 5!

1/ PLANT & SEED SUPPLIERS

Name
Address
City   State   Zip
Telephone   Fax
Web address
E-mail
Comments:

Name
Address
City   State   Zip
Telephone   Fax
Web address
E-mail
Comments:

Name
Address
City   State   Zip
Telephone   Fax
Web address
E-mail
Comments:

Name
Address
City   State   Zip
Telephone   Fax
Web address
E-mail
Comments:

Name

Address

City   State   Zip

Telephone   Fax

Web address

E-mail

Comments:

Name

Address

City   State   Zip

Telephone   Fax

Web address

E-mail

Comments:

Name

Address

City   State   Zip

Telephone   Fax

Web address

E-mail

Comments:

Name

Address

City   State   Zip

Telephone   Fax

Web address

E-mail

Comments:

Name _____
Address _____
City _____ State _____ Zip _____
Telephone _____ Fax _____
Web address _____
E-mail _____
Comments: _____
_____
_____

Name _____
Address _____
City _____ State _____ Zip _____
Telephone _____ Fax _____
Web address _____
E-mail _____
Comments: _____
_____
_____

Name _____
Address _____
City _____ State _____ Zip _____
Telephone _____ Fax _____
Web address _____
E-mail _____
Comments: _____
_____
_____
_____

Name _____
Address _____
City _____ State _____ Zip _____
Telephone _____ Fax _____
Web address _____ E-mail _____
Comments: _____
_____
_____

Fact: In the U.S. two out of three households
are involved in gardening

2 / EQUIPMENT SUPPLIERS

Name

Address

City   State   Zip

Telephone   Fax

Web address

E-mail

Comments:

Name

Address

City   State   Zip

Telephone   Fax

Web address

E-mail

Comments:

Name

Address

City   State   Zip

Telephone   Fax

Web address

E-mail

Comments:

Name

Address

City   State   Zip

Telephone   Fax

Web address

E-mail

Comments:

3 / MISCELLANEOUS

Name _____

Address _____

City _____ State _____ Zip _____

Telephone _____ Fax _____

Web address _____

E-mail _____

Comments: _____

_____

_____

Name _____

Address _____

City _____ State _____ Zip _____

Telephone _____ Fax _____

Web address _____

E-mail _____

Comments: _____

_____

_____

Name _____

Address _____

City _____ State _____ Zip _____

Telephone _____ Fax _____

Web address _____

E-mail _____

Comments: _____

_____

_____

Name _____

Address _____

City _____ State _____ Zip _____

Telephone _____ Fax _____

Web address _____

E-mail _____

Comments: _____

_____

_____

Weeds grow in *every* garden

GARDEN ORDERING RECORD

Who finds peace and contentment in the garden is happy for life

HERE is where you plan for your coming season's seeds and supplies. Be specific: Include the date, the name of your plant or seed supplier, the catalog **page** (if you order from a catalog), the **quantity** you order, the **name of the item**, the **cost** per item and the cost of the **total order** (see example below). You can keep track of multiple orders from several suppliers on this page. Keeping this information from season to season will be useful for reordering as well to provide a continuity to your garden. **(Note:** In your **Season's End** section later in this book, you return to this information to analyze your costs and results.)

MY GARDEN FOR THE YEAR
1999

Date	Supplier	Catalog Page	Quantity	Name of Item	Cost	Order Total
3/3	Great Plants	127	One Garden	Assortment Sunny Corner	29.99	
3/3	" "	132	One Garden	Assortment Real Shade	34.99	
				Total		$64.98
4/2	High Nursery	—	1	Burning Bush	9.99	
"	" "	—	1	Red Maple	19.99	
				Total		$29.98

In the example, the first two items were assortments ordered by mail; the second two were purchased directly from a nursery

MY GARDEN
FOR THE YEAR

_____

Date	Supplier	Catalog Page	Quantity	Name of Item	Cost	Order Total

Total for year $_____

MY GARDEN
FOR THE YEAR

_____

Date	Supplier	Catalog Page	Quantity	Name of Item	Cost	Order Total

Total for year $_____

 # MY GARDEN FOR THE YEAR

_____

Date	Supplier	Catalog Page	Quantity	Name of Item	Cost	Order Total

Total for year $ _____

 # MY GARDEN
FOR THE YEAR

_____

Date	Supplier	Catalog Page	Quantity	Name of Item	Cost	Order Total

Total for year $_____

MY GARDEN
FOR THE YEAR

_____

Date	Supplier	Catalog Page	Quantity	Name of Item	Cost	Order Total

Total for year $_____

MY GARDEN
FOR THE YEAR

Date	Supplier	Catalog Page	Quantity	Name of Item	Cost	Order Total

Total for year $_____

MY GARDEN
FOR THE YEAR

Date	Supplier	Catalog Page	Quantity	Name of Item	Cost	Order Total

Total for year $_____

GARDEN
PLANTING
NOTES

Here you can make notes for your coming garden to help you remember some of the things you want to do. For example:

Completed

₁ Plant flowers for shady areas [✓]

	Completed
1	
2/	
3/	
4/	
5/	
6/	
7/	
8/	
9/	
10/	

GETTING READY

	Completed
11/	
12/	
13/	
14/	
15/	
16/	
17/	
18/	
19/	
20/	
21/	
22/	
23/	
24/	
25/	
26/	
26/	
27/	
28/	

	Completed
29/	
30/	
31/	
32/	
33/	
34/	
35/	
36/	
37/	
38/	
39/	
40/	
41/	
42/	
43/	
44/	

GARDENING HINTS

Plan your next year's garden *this year*. Look at this year's garden and then decide what to improve upon. With your garden in front of you, you can also get a good idea of what you want to repeat again, or add to. Write up your plans in your **Garden Manager**.

SECTION 2

PLANTING
SEASON

🌱 How to use the Garden Grid

🌱 Year-by-year Garden Grid plans

🌱 Planting plan

🌱 Planning your garden or total landscape

🌱 Permanent planting information

🌱 Garden log & notebook

HOW TO USE
THE GARDEN GRID

Let your mind's eye dwell on that which is beautiful

WHETHER YOU are adding a designer flower garden to add a splash of color to a corner of your lot, adding a perennial border, doing a major landscaping or thinking of a vegetable garden, your garden should begin with a plan. It's up to you to decide:

How **big** you want your garden
What **shape** you want your garden to be
Its **location** and **direction** to the sun
What you want to plant and for what purpose

The best way to begin is to work out your plan on the following pages, utilizing this book's handy **Garden Grid Plan**. Also see *How to plan your garden or total landscape* (following).

The **Garden Grid Plan** is designed with a pre-marked scale of 1/2 inch, which most gardeners find easy to work with. You can make this scale equal whatever garden size you want, such as: 1/2 inch equals 1 foot of garden space. Some handy scales: 1/2 inch equals 1 foot. 1/2 inch equals 2 feet. 1/2 inch equals 3 feet

Once you have decided, write in the **Garden Grid Plan's** lower section your garden's size and the scale you want to work with. Also write in the year of your garden.

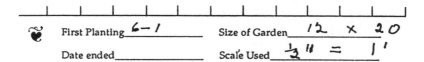

First Planting _6 – 1_   Size of Garden____ _12_ × _20_

Date ended_____   Scale Used____ $\frac{1}{2}$ " = _1 '_

Determine whether you want to work with your grid horizontally (for a wide garden) or vertically (for a longer garden). **Mark off** your grid with numbers. The garden *shown below* is laid out to be *vertical*. The gardener using this garden will have the side labeled **A** at the *bottom and toward him or her.* If you want a horizontal garden, you would have **B** side toward you. Number accordingly.

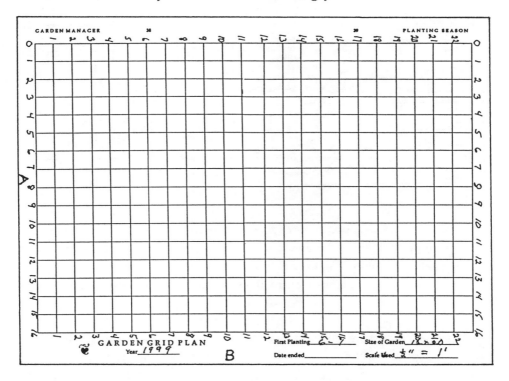

GARDEN GRID PLAN
Year _1999_

Plan before you plant. Work things out on paper, rather than on the ground. Planning will help you figure out how much space you will need for your garden and help you determine how many plants or packages of seeds you will need to buy. Try to figure out your **entire garden**, not just a small segment.

*In garden design, as in all the arts,
simplicity is the sign of perfection*

For example, let's say your garden will be **16 x 22** feet. Since **each grid square** equals **1 foot** of garden, you will fill up most of the two-page **Garden Grid Plan**. (If you need *more space*, you can have a *different scale*, such as *1/2 inch equals 2 feet*, or, you can use **more pages** by simply dividing your garden up into "plots," in which each book page equals one plot.)

In the example below, you will be working out plans for a vegetable garden on a typical **two-page** grid plan. In this space, you will have a **number of plantings**. For example, let's say you want to get in carrots and lettuce. You have determined that you want two rows of carrots (each row 16 feet wide, leaving half foot at the edge) and one row of lettuce). Though you will not be using all your seed in this *first planting*, you can mark your **Garden Grid Plan** as follows:

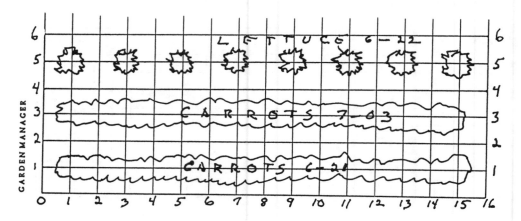

Note : you will be having two dates of plantings of carrots. You also can plant successive plantings of both carrots and lettuce. Note that on the leaf lettuce that you may wish to harvest by cutting back to the crowns, rather than by pulling out the entire plant. That way, in time, the plants will sprout again. (You'll want to record this, too!)

This is an example only. Few people will have perfect square or rectangular gardens — most have various shapes including curves or ovals, especially when planting flower or other decorative gardens. You can use the grid to design this this, too.

Two other items:

1/ Be certain to mark on your Planting Plan the date when you planted your seeds or bulbs. Also record the estimated time of har-

vest or when the plants will produce blossoms or reach maturity
(from your grower).

2/ Record every **instruction** included with your seeds or plants in
your **Permanent Planting Information.** You'll find that keeping information will give you good records to refer to and will help you avoid
difficulties later on.

In your planning on the following grids, try working with some
new ideas in your garden. Order plants you have had success with
in the past and like to harvest, but don't hesitate to try a few new
ones just for *fun*.

These just may turn out to be some of your future favorites.

❦ GARDENING HINTS

Plan before you plant. In your Garden Manager, organize your planting
schedule by date and write this down by date or season. Note the planting
times that are part of the instructions on your seed packet or plant.

Plant the tallest crops at the back of the garden; the shortest toward the front,
where they will receive the most sunlight. As you graduate the plants from
tallest to shortest, note which plants will need the most sun or do well in partial
sun. Observe where you will get the most sunshine.

Think of a second, and even a third, planting. Be certain to note this in your
planning section of your **Garden Manager.**

Check your garden soil at the beginning of the season. Remember it should not
only contain good loam, but sand, clay and humis. Humis can be added by
tilling or spading in leaves or grass clippings from your lawn.

Add a landscaping of flowers around your vegetable garden to have a bright
touch.

The gardener who says it cannot be done
should not interrupt the person actually doing it

HOW TO PLAN YOUR GARDEN OR TOTAL LANDSCAPE

By Leah Peterson
Washington County Master Gardener
Washington County, Minnesota

Step 1:

1. Draw your house and property line on a grid
2. Locate your trees and hardscapes, such as driveways, walks and patios
3. Note *North, South, East* and *West* on your grid. Also note sun, shade and soil conditions.

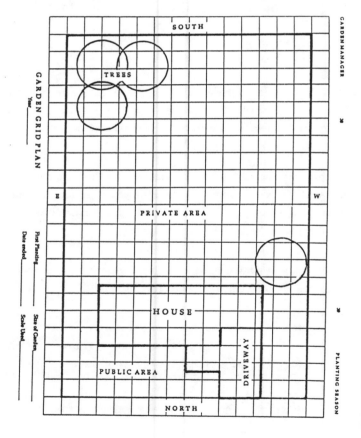

For example:

  North garden - entry - mostly light shade
  East garden - shady due to neighbor's house
  West garden - shady due to neighbor's house
  South garden - sunny

Step 2: The Goose Egg Study

1. List your wants and needs for your landscape. *Example of needs:*
*Want a vegetable garden *Want flower beds with perennials *Don't
want to work too hard *Need screen from east neighbor and patio
*Need play area for kids *Want patio and privacy from neighbors
*Want clothes line

2. Put tracing paper over your grid plan and with a pencil experi-
ment with what you want your landscape to provide.

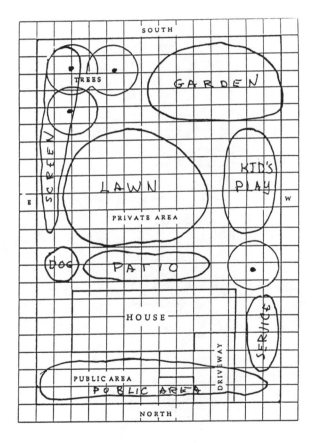

Notes: The landscaping of your property can include different types
of gardens. Main entry gardens enhance the front door area, walkway
and driveway. Realtors call this "curb appeal."

- More and more designers are using groundcovers rather than lawn
  or turf.
- Color is often found in containers near the front door rather than in
  extensive flower plantings

- The new American garden look uses groundcovers and shrubs for permanent entry plantings
- Look for year-around interest with plantings
- Remember that your entry garden is viewed in all seasons and summer foliage is only three or four months. Fall color and winter interest is essential.
- Take a picture of your front entry and have it enlarged. Then use tracing paper to draw in heights and widths of plantings.
- The New American Garden features different specialty gardens such as butterfly gardens, cutting garden, perennial, wildlife, herb, kitchen, children's, fragrance, bog, water, prairie wild flowers, shade, bulbs, or is built around a special kind of flower such as a lily garden.

Step 3:

Some plans
and examples:

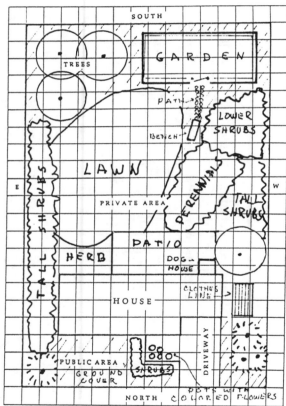

Notes:

Gardens are planned for herbs, vegetables and flowers

Patio and kids area — shared by dog

Gate and path, with "interest" specimen trees or large shrubs chosen with four-season interest

Entry garden, evergreens and massed flowers and groundcover

Small turf area means low maintenance

Shrubs provide privacy; add clothes line

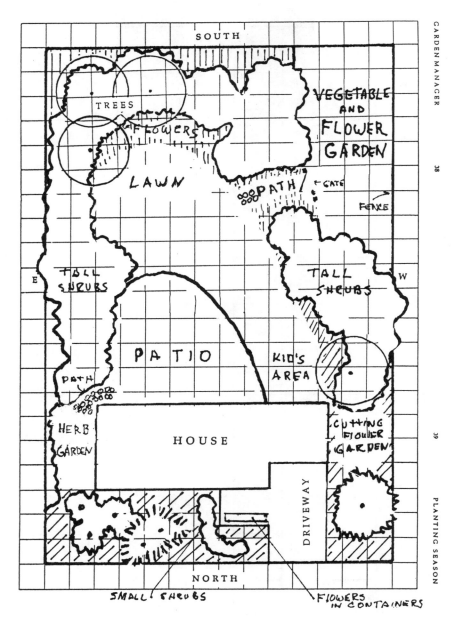

SOUTH

GARDEN MANAGER

38

TREES

FLOWERS

VEGETABLE
AND
FLOWER
GARDEN

LAWN

PATH

GATE

FENCE

E   TALL
SHRUBS

TALL
SHRUBS

W

PATIO

KID'S
AREA

PATH

HOUSE

HERB
GARDEN

CUTTING
FLOWER
GARDEN

39

DRIVEWAY

PLANTING SEASON

NORTH

SMALL SHRUBS

FLOWERS
IN CONTAINERS

Plan Two

Herb, vegetable and flower gardens
Patio and lawn area for kids and dog
"Interest" with garden and gate
Tall shade screens for privacy
Entry garden with specimen trees and low shrubs
Evergreens and shrubs — four-season interest — also food and shelter for birds.

GARDEN GRID PLAN
Year_____

First Planting_____   Size of Garden_____

Date ended_____   Scale Used_____

GARDEN GRID PLAN

Year_____

First Planting_____   Size of Garden_____

Date ended_____   Scale Used_____

GARDEN GRID PLAN
Year_____

First Planting_____   Size of Garden_____

Date ended_____   Scale Used_____

GARDEN GRID PLAN

Year_____

First Planting_____   Size of Garden_____

Date ended_____   Scale Used_____

GARDEN GRID PLAN

Year_____

First Planting_____   Size of Garden_____

Date ended_____   Scale Used_____

GARDEN GRID PLAN
Year_____

First Planting_____   Size of Garden_____

Date ended_____   Scale Used_____

GARDEN GRID PLAN
Year_____

First Planting_____   Size of Garden_____

Date ended_____   Scale Used_____

GARDEN GRID PLAN
Year_____

First Planting_____   Size of Garden_____

Date ended_____   Scale Used_____

PLANTING PLAN

Everything is beautiful in its own time and way

WRITE below the information you need about each crop you plant. Your crop information should correlate with your **Garden Grid**. Include the exact name of your crop, the date you planted it, and the date of estimated maturity. For example:

Crop	Date Planted	Estimated Maturity
(A) Big Boy Melon	May 20	80 DAYS
(B) Sweet Pea	May 23	70 DAYS
(C) Great Tomato	May 26	65 Days

Crop	Date Planted	Estimated Maturity

Saying about some avid gardeners:
They could put a stick in the ground and it would grow

Crop	Date Planted	Estimated Maturity

Gardening is a higher form of life

Crop	Date Planted	Estimated Maturity

Crop	Date Planted	Estimated Maturity
_____	_____	_____
_____	_____	_____
_____	_____	_____
_____	_____	_____
_____	_____	_____
_____	_____	_____
_____	_____	_____
_____	_____	_____
_____	_____	_____
_____	_____	_____
_____	_____	_____
_____	_____	_____
_____	_____	_____
_____	_____	_____
_____	_____	_____
_____	_____	_____
_____	_____	_____

Be content. Big gardens mean big problems

Crop	Date Planted	Estimated Maturity
_____	_____	_____
_____	_____	_____
_____	_____	_____
_____	_____	_____
_____	_____	_____
_____	_____	_____
_____	_____	_____
_____	_____	_____
_____	_____	_____
_____	_____	_____
_____	_____	_____
_____	_____	_____
_____	_____	_____
_____	_____	_____
_____	_____	_____
_____	_____	_____
_____	_____	_____

Crop	Date Planted	Estimated Maturity
_____	_____	_____
_____	_____	_____
_____	_____	_____
_____	_____	_____
_____	_____	_____
_____	_____	_____
_____	_____	_____
_____	_____	_____
_____	_____	_____
_____	_____	_____
_____	_____	_____
_____	_____	_____
_____	_____	_____
_____	_____	_____
_____	_____	_____

Too much of a good thing for a gardener can be wonderful

Crop	Date Planted	Estimated Maturity

To it! Your garden won't get done unless you up and do it

PERMANENT PLANTING INFORMATION

Gardening can teach you if you let it

HERE YOU KEEP the basic information from each seed packet or bulb that you will need later on. This should include the plant name, how big a row the crop will plant, the estimated maturity in days, and instructions on planting and harvesting. For example:

> (C) LETTUCE, Green Goddess (45 Days)
> Sows 25', plant successively each 2 weeks
> for repeat harvests. Sow $\frac{1}{4}$"–$\frac{1}{2}$" apart
> + thinly. Thin seedlings to 4" to 12"
> apart. (Use seedlings for early salad!)

Plant   **Basic information**

_____

_____

_____

_____

Plant   Basic information

_____

_____

_____

_____

_____

_____

_____

_____

_____

_____

_____

_____

_____

_____

_____

_____

_____

Plant   **Basic information**

Dirt is a gift to the true gardener

Plant   **Basic information**

Plant　　　　　　**Basic information**

When all else fails — read the planting instructions

Plant   **Basic information**

_____

_____

_____

_____

_____

_____

_____

_____

_____

_____

_____

_____

_____

_____

_____

_____

Plant   **Basic information**

_____

_____

_____

_____

_____

_____

_____

_____

_____

_____

_____

_____

_____

_____

Who never strives in the garden never learns anything new

Plant   **Basic information**

_____

_____

_____

_____

_____

_____

_____

_____

_____

_____

_____

_____

GARDENING HINTS

Check with planting charts for instructions on watering, shade tolerance and sunshine needed. Also check watering instructions since overwatering is often a mistake.

Keep a record of where plants were purchased, how much they cost and if they were healthy.

GARDEN LOG AND NOTEBOOK

Gardening can teach you if you let it

HERE YOU CAN KEEP track of the general work you do in your garden. You can have a permanent record from year to year on soil samples and how you treat your soil. Here's the place to keep track of tilling, raking, fertilizing, thinning or weeding. Here you can handle the measurement or progress of your plants, so that you can make yearly comparisons. Start with a date.

5-20: Got new soil sample analyzed.
5-21: Hired a power tiller to turn over garden. Added leaves + clippings.
5-22: Raked garden. Planted 2 rows of lettuce.

_____

_____

_____

_____

_____

_____

_____

_____

_____

_____

_____

_____

_____

_____

_____

_____

_____

One is not born a gardener. You become one

Memories grow from days like this in the garden

Dreams have power for gardeners

_____

_____

_____

_____

_____

_____

_____

_____

_____

_____

_____

_____

_____

_____

_____

_____

_____

_____

If not now in the garden — when?

GARDENING HINTS

Enhance your garden's enjoyment by adding a chair, glider, or set of chairs nearby, overlooking it. This will make your garden a relaxing area for you and your friends to enjoy as well as to make it a focus of part of your outdoor living. Think of adding bird baths and feeders for your feathered friends and a cookout area for you and your family.

Organize your garden to save time and effort. If possible, locate it near your house or garage where you keep your tools. Think of having a special toolshed, either separate or as a part of the garage, where you can keep all your tools. Be certain your garden is accessible.

SECTION 3

HARVEST
SECTION

❦ **Harvest records
& comments**

❦ **Notes for next season**

**In gardening, as in life, those who do
not know their history are likely to repeat it**

HARVEST RECORDS

**Reflect on your blessings,
of which every gardener has many**

YOU WILL WANT to keep a record of how well your garden did. Some plantings may have gotten off to a superb start and bloomed well. Others may not have done so well as you had hoped, and you will want to be watchful of these in the future. You will want to have a record of **when** you harvested your crop (or, if it is flowers, when it came into full bloom), the **name** of the crop, and a quantitative **description** of the mature crop. It's a good idea, too, to write down anything **affecting your crop**, either good or bad, so that you know what happened. Here's an example:

Harvest date	name of crop	analysis

6-08-99 (Bloom) Gold Marigold. First Sprouts 7 days. Plant height: 2½'. Good color + bloom. Check length of bloom.

8-12-99 (Harvest) Big tomato. 63 days to bear first fruit. Good taste, firm. Good bearer. Av. weight: 8 oz.

Harvest date   **name of crop**   **analysis**

_____

_____

_____

_____

_____

_____

_____

_____

_____

_____

_____

_____

_____

_____

_____

_____

The littlest things make the biggest differences

Harvest date   **name of crop**   **analysis**

_____

_____

_____

_____

_____

_____

_____

_____

_____

_____

_____

_____

_____

_____

The Lord does not subtract from your allotted days on earth
those that you spend in your garden

Harvest date   **name of crop**   **analysis**

_____

_____

_____

_____

_____

_____

_____

_____

_____

_____

_____

_____

_____

_____

Gardening is the proper path for the soul

Harvest date	name of crop		analysis

They can because they think they can

Harvest date	name of crop	analysis

Rise and shine for your garden's doing fine

Harvest date	name of crop	analysis

Two rules for the veteran gardener: Rule 1/ Don't sweat
the small stuff Rule 2/ It's all small stuff

Harvest date   **name of crop**   **analysis**

_____

_____

_____

_____

_____

_____

_____

_____

_____

_____

_____

_____

_____

_____

_____

If your garden seems to cost too much, think of money like fertilizer:
It's only any good when it gets spread around

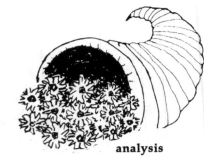

Harvest date   **name of crop**   **analysis**

_____

_____

_____

_____

_____

_____

_____

_____

_____

_____

_____

_____

GARDENING HINTS

Add gardening books to your list of presents to give and to receive for yourself and your friends. Give a **Garden Manager** to a fellow gardener. For a step-by-step gardening adventure through the best of gardens in England, see the "Gardener's London" chapter in **London for the Independent Traveler** at your favorite bookstore or available directly from the publisher Marlor Press (*$12.95, plus $3.00 postage & handling)*

N O T E S   F O R
N E X T   S E A S O N

Beauty is in the details

HERE you can jot down some thoughts for the next season. It's important to work with this section as you think of things you want to remember: write them down right away. You'd be surprised at how useful this section can be in a few months. Start with a one or two word description and then summarize. Like this:

Early Seeds: try seeds in trays grown inside for later transplant.
Compost: Get a compost bin and compost grass clippings!

Think spring and what you can do
ahead of time

NOTES FOR NEXT SEASON

_____

_____

_____

_____

_____

_____

_____

_____

_____

_____

_____

_____

_____

_____

_____

_____

_____

Gardening euphemism: "I am experiencing different success rates."

If you like rainbows, put up with a little rain

NOTES FOR NEXT SEASON

Why hurry? Gardening is a labor of love

_____

_____

_____

_____

_____

_____

_____

_____

_____

_____

_____

_____

_____

_____

Remember that there's always next season

NOTES FOR NEXT SEASON

_____

_____

_____

_____

_____

_____

_____

_____

_____

_____

_____

_____

_____

_____

_____

_____

A carefully prepared journal enjoyably draws the gardening seasons together and
melds the gardener closer to the garden

It's always fair weather when
good gardeners get together

_____

_____

_____

_____

_____

_____

_____

_____

_____

_____

_____

_____

_____

_____

GARDENING HINT

Flowers can be used creatively throughout a landscape. They add not only color and beauty but provide a sense of celebration, letting the gardener exercise a special creativity with their color, shape and fragrance. In small groupings or in coordinated designs, they can bring an area alive.

SECTION 4:

SEASON'S END

🌢 Analysis of my garden's harvest

🌢 What I want to do next season

ANALYSIS OF
MY GARDEN'S
HARVEST

Good gardens draw one closer to nature

AFTER THE LAST BLOOMS have faded and the last plants harvested and your garden lying dormant, now is the time to sit back and take a look at your overall results. In this calm you can objectively compare what you got with what you wanted. Be specific, and, if you wish, problem solve for each planting.

Marigolds. Good bloom + Color.
Find sunnier spot. Start indoors
for earlier start.

Tomatoes. Great crop — but all
at once. Solution — early and late
maturing plants. Plant successively —
not all at once. Begin some indoors

In gardening, go for excellence — not perfection

❧ Analysis for year

_____

_____

_____

_____

_____

_____

_____

_____

_____

_____

_____

_____

_____

_____

_____

Being a happy gardner is not so much the absence
of problems as the ability to deal with them

❦ Analysis for year

_____

🌱 Analysis for year

_____

_____

_____

_____

_____

_____

_____

_____

_____

_____

_____

_____

_____

_____

_____

_____

_____

_____

If it grows — it grows

❧ Analysis for year

_____

❧ Analysis for year

_____

_____

_____

_____

_____

_____

_____

_____

_____

_____

_____

_____

_____

_____

_____

_____

_____

This season create the garden of your dreams.

🍃 Analysis for year

_____

_____

_____

_____

_____

_____

_____

_____

_____

_____

_____

_____

_____

_____

_____

_____

_____

_____

_____

_____

 As long as you keep a sense of perspective, you're ahead of the game

❦ Analysis for year

_____

_____

_____

_____

_____

_____

_____

_____

_____

_____

_____

_____

_____

_____

_____

_____

The surer you garden the farther you'll go

❦ Analysis for year

_____

_____

_____

_____

_____

_____

_____

_____

_____

_____

_____

_____

_____

_____

_____

_____

Love what you do in your garden
— or don't do it

🍂 Analysis for year

_____

_____

_____

_____

_____

_____

_____

_____

_____

_____

_____

_____

_____

_____

_____

_____

_____

Don't live tomorrow until it arrives

GARDENING
INFORMATION

There are many sources of gardening information. A gardener can check libraries, bookstores, and garden centers for gardening books. If you are an internet browser, use a search engine to "gardens" or "gardening" to find a variety of information.

One of the best sources of free gardening information is from your County Extension Office. There is also a Master Gardener program in 45 states, the District of Columbia and some Canadian Provinces. Volunteers who train as Master Gardeners staff horticulture hotlines, coordinate environmental and planting projects, run demonstration gardens, do research, manage some existing public gardens, work with school groups and other special populations, publish newsletters, and broadcast radio and television programs.

To become a Master Gardener, for example under the Michigan Master Gardener Program (offered by the Michigan State University Extension) applicants attend classes in their county, learn basic horticultural principles and environmentally sound gardening practices. They then provide a minimum of 40 hours of volunteer service to their community. For information about your local Master Gardening program contact your county Cooperative Extension Office in the U.S. or the Canadian Ministry of Agriculture.

Master Gardener programs are coordinated under Master Gardeners International, 424 North River Drive, Woodstock, VA 22664. If you write to them for information, include a self-addressed stamped envelope. The E-mail address is mgic@capaccess.org. You can get a list of contact persons and telephone numbers for each state and participating province. Your County Extension Office will be able to inform you about the Master Gardener program in your area.

    🌱   You can't have a garden today by only dreaming about tomorrow

WHAT I
WANT TO DO
NEXT SEASON

HERE is where you lay plans for your next season's garden — while memories and dreams of this season's are still on your mind. A little more garden space? Make your *Garden Grid Plan* well in advance of planting season? Get the garden tilled a little earlier this year? Analyze the soil for balance? Order plants a little earlier? Get them started sooner? All these can be on your "to do" list next season — if you begin to make plans next year. Be specific.

Next Season

_____

_____

_____

_____

The journey is sometimes
better than the destination

Next Season

_____

_____

_____

_____

_____

_____

_____

_____

_____

_____

_____

_____

_____

_____

_____

_____

Discovery awaits in your garden

Next Season

_____

_____

_____

_____

_____

_____

_____

_____

_____

_____

_____

_____

_____

_____

_____

Rise early at least once to see the sunrise in your garden

Next Season

_____

If your eyes are open you will always discover something new
and delightful in your garden

Next Season

_____

_____

_____

_____

_____

_____

_____

_____

_____

_____

_____

_____

_____

_____

_____

_____

_____

You are a true gardener if you see something you must have
when you visit someone else's garden

GARDENING
FRIENDS

NAME _____

ADDRESS _____

CITY _____ STATE _____ ZIP _____

TELEPHONE _____ E-MAIL _____

NAME _____

ADDRESS _____

CITY _____ STATE _____ ZIP _____

TELEPHONE _____ E-MAIL _____

NAME _____

ADDRESS _____

CITY _____ STATE _____ ZIP _____

TELEPHONE _____ E-MAIL _____

NAME _____

ADDRESS _____

CITY _____ STATE _____ ZIP _____

TELEPHONE _____ E-MAIL _____

Gardening friends can add to the fun of gardening

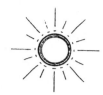

NAME _____

ADDRESS _____

CITY _____ STATE _____ ZIP _____

TELEPHONE _____ E-MAIL _____

NAME _____

ADDRESS _____

CITY _____ STATE _____ ZIP _____

TELEPHONE _____ E-MAIL _____

NAME _____

ADDRESS _____

CITY _____ STATE _____ ZIP _____

TELEPHONE _____ E-MAIL _____

NAME _____

ADDRESS _____

CITY _____ STATE _____ ZIP _____

TELEPHONE _____ E-MAIL _____

Mark of a good gardener: Wherever you go, people give you
something from their garden

 # MARLOR PRESS BOOKS

LONDON FOR THE INDEPENDENT TRAVELER — Find the best of London's historic palaces, castles and fascinating places at your own pace with this acclaimed guidebook. Includes a three-day guide to splendid English gardens in a special chapter, **Gardener's London**. Complete with maps, charts and illustrations — everything you need to get around on your own. "Practically holds your hand " *Conde Nast's Traveler*. Only **$12.95**

GARDEN MANAGER — Any gardener will find this five year organizer and planner fun all year around and worth a place on a workbench. In four sections, **Garden Manager** helps gardeners develop a plan for their gardens, keep track of what they grow, and analyze their gardens for better results. Complete with *Garden Grid Plans*. A great gift for a fellow gardener. (Special discounts for quantity orders from garden clubs). Only **$15.95**

COMPLETE TRIP DIARY — This low cost journal and trip organizer has saved many a vacation. Keeps track of schedules and daily expenses (never get caught short again) as well as contains two full pages for you to journal in each day of your vacation (up to three weeks). Lots of helpful stuff — a terrifically handy little book for any gardener on a trip or vacation. Only **$8.95**

GOING ABROAD — Here's a humorous, but practical guide that tells step by step how to use the many kinds of toilets throughout the world. For any gardener taking a trip abroad, this can be a real, er, life saver. Shows how to use European and Asian toilets, from Europe's street corner (but baffling) biffies to the ubiquitous squat toilet. Gives techniques on squatting, aiming and other really necessary stuff travelers may never have thought about, but should. A most useful book for any traveler, and a great gift book for anyone going abroad. A must for gardeners wherever they, er, go. Only **$12.95**

Marlor Press books are available in most bookstores and may also be ordered directly from the publisher by phone during business hours at 1 - 800 - 669-4908 with your Visa or Master Card number. ($3 for postage and handling for the first book, $1 for each additional book).

 **MARLOR PRESS**
4304 Brigadoon Drive   Saint Paul, MN 55126

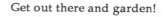
Get out there and garden!